Ghostly Encounters

IRELAND, ENGLAND, and SPAIN

Rosemary Butler

Sun on Earth™ Books
Heathsville, Virginia

Published by Sun on Earth™ Books

www.sunonearth.com

Illustrations by the author.

Publisher's Cataloging-in-Publication Data
Butler, Rosemary.
Ghostly encounters: Ireland, England, and Spain
/ Rosemary Butler. — 1st ed.
p. cm.
1. Folklore—Ghosts. 2. Ireland—Travel.
3. England—Travel. 4. Spain—Travel.
5. England—History. 6. Ireland—History. I. Title.

BF1472 .B88 2010 133.1—dc21

Library of Congress Control Number: 2010924150

ISBN-13: 978-1-883378-01-1
ISBN-10: 1-883378-01-X

I used to think I'd never see,
In truthful actuality,
A banshee, wraith, or spectral ghost,
An apparition, or at most
A shadow moving late at night,
Forward and back or left and right.
But now I think that I can boast,
I've finally seen a real-life ghost.

ROSEMARY BUTLER

Table of Contents

INTRODUCTION

The first time I thought seriously about ghosts was in the Philippines, when our friend Beezie told my husband Charles and me about a ghost in her California home. Until then, I had been a disbeliever in the supernatural.

When Beezie told us the story of her ghost, she and her husband Jim were sitting with us in the living room of our house on Clark Air Force Base in the Philippines. The house had been built shortly after the Spanish-American War, and would be eventually buried in volcanic ash, in 1991, from the eruption of nearby Mt. Pinatubo. The thick covering of ash must have presented an eerie sight, much like Beezie's ghost.

When Beezie saw her ghost, she and Jim were living on a hilltop above Hollywood, in an Art Deco house that had been built by a film director, then deceased. Not long after they moved into the house, Beezie became aware of strange sounds, sudden movements of chairs, and the rustle of draperies in an adjoining room. Finally, the cause of these mysterious manifestations appeared to her in plain sight—but only to her, not to Jim nor any of their friends. Beezie thought the ghost might be the film director returning to haunt her, until she and Jim moved away.

To Beezie, the ghost was more annoying than frightening, especially when it would appear at their cocktail parties or dinners. Then, it would taunt her by bending over her guests and waving its arms. After one party, when Beezie had had more than enough of its antics, she shouted at the ghost, "GET OUT OF MY HOUSE AND DON'T EVER COME BACK!" That was the last time she saw it.

Beezie told her ghost story so convincingly, that I was no longer such a skeptic when it came to ghosts. After that day, I often thought of ghosts appearing in places where Charles and I had lived—in Europe, Asia, and the United States—during his twenty-year career as a Civil Engineer Corps officer in the U.S. Navy. We traveled extensively and encountered a few ghosts in England and Spain, but it was not until we began visiting Ireland in the early 1970s that we found ghosts galore.

We had considered visiting Ireland when we lived in northwest Spain, which, like the Emerald Isle, has a Celtic heritage and a landscape that is also many shades of green. But our interest was truly aroused when we read in a guidebook that our surname, Butler, was scattered around the island in rather prominent ways.

Who could resist visiting the land where Butlers had played such a notable role? We flew to Ireland that very same year and have vacationed there a dozen times since. Besides finding Butler stately homes and castles, and even a Butler Society, we also found a Butler ghost—with an elegant title, too!

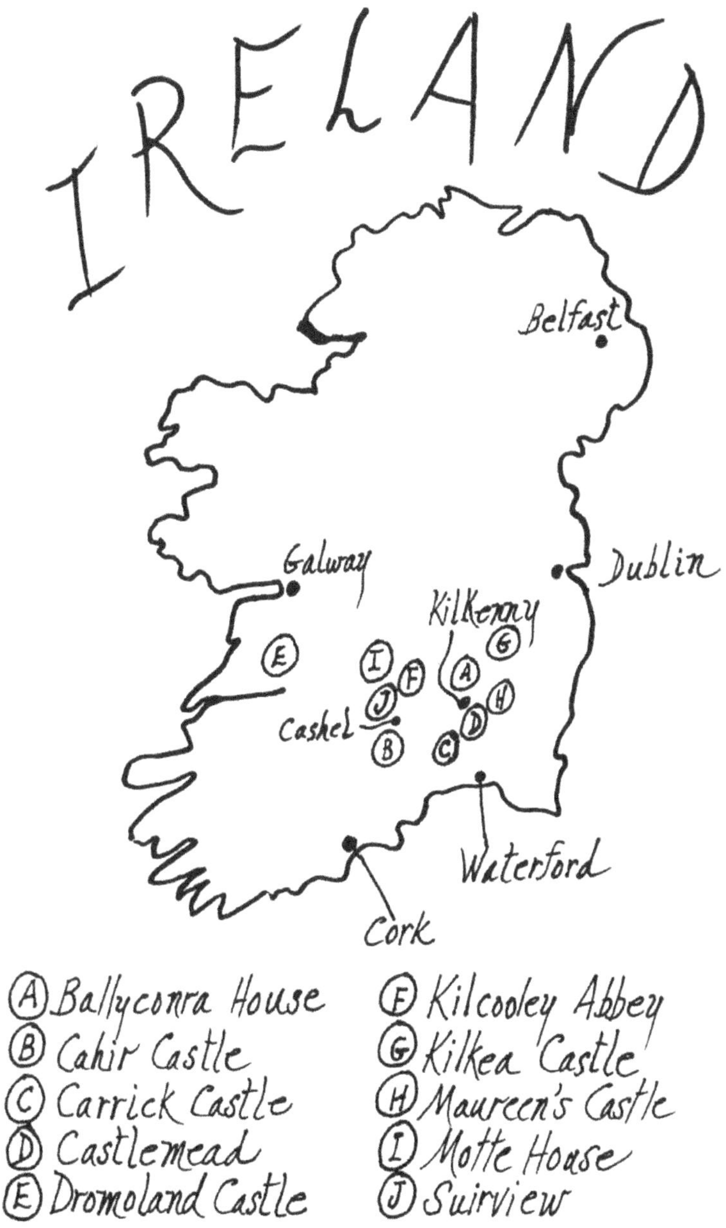
IRELAND
Belfast
Galway
Dublin
Kilkenny
Cashel
Waterford
Cork
A Ballyconra House
B Cahir Castle
C Carrick Castle
D Castlemead
E Dromoland Castle
F Kilcooley Abbey
G Kilkea Castle
H Maureen's Castle
I Motte House
J Suirview

THE WANDERING GHOST OF KILKEA

Kilkea Castle

Before I tell you about the first Irish ghost that I encountered, a word about the two most powerful families on the Emerald Isle in medieval and Tudor times—the Fitzgeralds and the Butlers. Both families owned a great deal of land and built many castles. One of these, which belonged to the Fitzgeralds, was Kilkea Castle. It was turned into a hotel several decades ago. The hotel was called simply Kilkea Castle (pronounced "kill-key"). We stayed there for the first time in the early 1970s.

One thing I read about Kilkea Castle that caught my interest was its being haunted by the ghost of Garrett Og Fitzgerald, the Eleventh Earl of Kildare, who lived there in the sixteenth century. Known as the Wizard Earl, he is said to have practiced magic in his room, located in the castle's highest tower. I wondered if his ghost would welcome us or not to this Fitzgerald home, since Charles and I were of the rival Butler clan.

The rivalry between the Butlers and the Fitzgeralds endured for several centuries. Both families were of Anglo-Norman origin, and although several marriages took place between them over the years, they were most often arranged to settle disputes over the boundaries of their respective landholdings. There were frequent armed clashes across their borders.

The clashes culminated during the reign of Queen Elizabeth I, when the last private war on British soil was fought in 1565 between Thomas Butler, Tenth Earl of Ormond, and Gerald Fitzgerald, Fifteenth Earl of Desmond—at Affane, near the Blackwater River in County Waterford. The Earl of Desmond was wounded in the battle and taken to Waterford as a captive by the victorious Earl of Ormond.

Our first night at Kilkea Castle, we dined late in the evening, which was the norm for Irish diners, as it was for us. Having lived in Spain, we were accustomed to dining at such hours. After dinner, we wandered around the hallways until we came to the front desk, where we found the receptionist.

Remembering that the castle was supposed to be haunted, I asked her, "Could we see the room where Garrett Og

Fitzgerald, the Wizard Earl, practiced his magic? I know it's late, but we're curious to see the room."

She motioned to a bellboy, who looked about the age of ten, and told him, "Take the American visitors up the tower to see the Wizard Earl's room."

I have never seen such a reluctant boy. Not a word from him, but his body language spoke, "NO! PLEASE, NO!"

With an oil lantern in his quivering hands, the bellboy led us up a winding stone stair, which seemed to grow steeper and narrower the farther up we climbed.

When we reached the top, the bellboy paused before opening a narrow door. Inside was a small, dark room. Because of the faint lantern light, all I remember seeing was a single bed surrounded by shadows that seemed to sway. But an odd feeling came over me, as though I were being watched.

Was the room haunted? Perhaps. Led by the nervous bellboy, we hurried back down the winding stair, constantly touching the tower's limestone wall to keep from tripping on the treacherous stone treads. We never saw the bellboy again. He probably thought we might wish to repeat the climb.

To reach our hotel room, we had to climb another stone stair. It had wide steps and was lighted, not like the stair in the tower. Then we walked down a long hallway to our corner room. I quickly fell asleep.

An hour or so later, I was suddenly awake. I had heard a sound—someone slowly walking up a nearby stair, wearing heavy boots. Then the sound stopped outside our room. I was so frightened, I froze, unable to move or even speak. Silence. Finally, I fell fitfully asleep.

The next day, as we strolled along a path below our room, I looked up to our window, high above. There was a narrow tower nearby. It rose from where we stood to the castle's roof. In front of us, we saw that the tower's doorway had been completely blocked so that no one could go inside.

When we returned to our room, we checked the wall where a door to the tower could have been. There was no door, but we knew the tower was right outside. I was sure that the sound of heavy boots had come from a stair inside *this* tower. Yet the entrance to the tower was blocked.

That night, we decided to have cocktails before going to the castle's dining room. The receptionist said, "The cocktail lounge is at the base of the tower you climbed last night."

When we entered the lounge, we found a small bar, and opposite it, another doorway and a bench. Expecting a few hotel guests to be joining us, and a barman to serve us, we were surprised to find that no one was here. Charles and I sat on the bench waiting for the barman to appear.

Feeling chilly in this lonely place, I asked Charles, "Would you mind going up to the room for my cardigan?" He gallantly agreed, even knowing he would have to climb the long stone stairway to our floor.

When he left, I was all alone—a Butler alone in a Fitzgerald tower—and I was shivering. The base of a medieval tower, I realized, should be cool, especially on this late fall night. Then, all at once, I was more than chilly. A blanket of very cold air silently enveloped me. It could have come through either doorway. I saw nothing, but I felt an icy presence. Was it the Wizard Earl protesting our visit to his study the night before? All I can say is that when Charles returned, I told him, "Let's go to the dining room and order cocktails *there*!"

Years later, Charles and I returned to Kilkea Castle. In the meantime, many changes had been made. Outside, a spa and other buildings had been added to the grounds, as well as a garden with beautiful pathways. Inside, the reception area had been moved to a new location, and a large sitting room had been created in its place. Beyond, and almost out of sight, we saw the winding stair that went up the tower to the Wizard Earl's room. Now the stair had been roped off.

The next morning, we stood in the new sitting room and stared at the rope. Since no one was in sight, we decided to slip under it and climb the stair a second time.

At the top, sunshine lighted the door to the Wizard Earl's room. Charles cautiously opened it, and we found the room stuffed with brooms and pails and mops. The Wizard Earl could not work his magic there.

"His ghost must have grown discouraged and fled the castle, never to return," I suggested. Charles agreed.

Outside, near the foot of the tower, we met an elderly laborer who was eager to chat with us. He pointed out, near the top of the tower, a carved coat of arms that we had not seen before.

This seemed the perfect opportunity for me to tell him, "We climbed that tower this morning and looked into the Wizard Earl's room. But there was no sign of him at all."

"Ah, but the Wizard Earl is still around," said the elderly man. "He has been seen at night lingering outside his tower room, and he also roams the halls. 'Tis said that hotel guests do see him from time to time, but never in the daylight hours."

That night, we left our room for dinner about nine o'clock. While Charles locked the door, I glanced down the dimly lit hall. For one moment, I was startled to see a gray shadow, which faded, and then quickly disappeared. I had just seen my first Irish ghost.

THE GHOST IN THE TOWER

DROMOLAND CASTLE

Charles and I started staying at Dromoland Castle, County Clare, in the 1970s, and through the years we have stayed in many different rooms in this storybook hotel. On one of our earliest visits, we stayed in a room at the top of a polygonal tower. It turned out to be a memorable experience.

On our arrival, Eamon, the head hall porter, who had worked at Dromoland Castle for many years, took our luggage and said most graciously, "Please, follow me." He was such a distinguished gentleman, it was easy to mistake him for the owner of this vast and intriguing place.

Eamon led us down long corridors to a dark room at the foot of a spiral stair, which rose through a claustrophobic tower.

"May I precede you?" he asked with a slight bow. "Please do," we said.

So Eamon, loaded with luggage, led the way. The steps were so steep, the treads so narrow, and the tower walls so close, I feared Eamon would not be able to manage our luggage, plus himself, all the way up the forty-nine steps.

At the top, he unlocked the door to our room (the only one in the tower), and ushered us in. With its many windows, the room offered splendid views of chimneys and other towers, as well as a lake and the wooded grounds beyond.

When Eamon left, we sat down to rest in the two easy chairs that faced the door. We were exhausted from our long day's drive. Then, suddenly, the door—which Eamon had carefully closed—opened slowly, mysteriously, and deliberately. But no one was there. We were too tired to even be startled. All I could say was, "Please, come in." As a response, we noticed only a cool draft from the stair.

At dinner that night, we considered the possibility that a ghost had entered our room. How else could we explain the opening of our door—with no one there?

When we saw Eamon the next day and described the incident, it came as no surprise to him. In a lowered voice he said, "Yes, other Dromoland Castle guests have felt the presence of the ghost who lives in your tower. In fact, one lady guest refused to return to the room you now occupy, after feeling the presence. It is well-known by the hotel staff that the room in that tower is…haunted."

THE INTERRUPTED MEAL

Maureen's Castle

On almost every visit to Ireland, Charles and I spent a whole day in County Kilkenny. There, a dear friend accompanied us to places all over the county, places she knew would interest us.

I had already alerted Margaret to my interest in the spirit world, so on this particular day, she said, "We are going to visit Maureen, who lives in a castle not far from town. The original tower was attacked by Cromwell in the seventeenth century, and a new castle was built on its site."

Before we reached Maureen's castle, Margaret told us, "I know you will be especially interested in going there, not only because Maureen is most charming, but also because, at her castle, two mysterious things have taken place. The first one happened over two hundred years ago. One night, when the owner of the castle and his family were dining quietly together in the hall, they all heard the distant rattling of a coach pulled by four horses, the combination called a coach-and-four. This coach-and-four had been driving directly up the long, straight entrance lane, gradually growing louder as it drew closer and closer to the castle's main door."

Our friend continued: "The owner of the castle left the hall to see who had come to call. Just as he approached the front door, the sound of horses' hooves and carriage wheels abruptly stopped. When he opened the door, he looked out in amazement. There was nothing there. No coach-and-four, only the blackness of the night."

"The following night," Margaret said, "while the owner and his family dined, they heard again the clatter of horses' hooves and carriage wheels. So the owner left the hall to see who had come to call. And again, the noise stopped abruptly, just before he reached the door. And when he opened it, there was only the blackness of the night. This scenario happened night after night, and the whole family grew afraid, then annoyed. Finally, the owner made up his mind to stop the predictable ghostly noise."

"He hired workmen to block the entrance lane," continued Margaret, "so that the coach-and-four could never use that lane again. At the same time, he hired other workmen to construct a new entrance lane, so that it reached the main door from the side. Then he hired other workmen to build a gate and gatehouse at the beginning of the new entrance lane. Both gate and gatehouse were elaborate, castellated, and immense—and they discouraged the nightly visits, for the coach-and-four never came again."

Soon we were to drive past this gatehouse, through the entrance gate, and up the long, new entrance lane.

"Before we arrive at the castle," Margaret said, "I must tell you what Maureen saw in her drawing room a few years ago. She had just come into the room and stood by a window that overlooks the front lawn and the entrance lane. On the far side of the room is a huge gilt-framed mirror, probably brought by her ancestors from Italy a hundred years ago. As Maureen looked past the room's fine Victorian furnishings, to the mirror, she was startled to see a gentleman in fashionable nineteenth-century clothes walking *through* the adjacent wall. Then, as he stepped in front of the mirror, he faded away, as though swallowed by the glass. Maureen was calm but incredulous at first. How could the gentleman ghost come through the wall?"

"Then one day," Margaret explained, "while Maureen was looking at an old sketch of the drawing room, she saw that there had once been a door exactly where the ghost had stepped through the wall. Apparently, the gentleman ghost had once lived in the castle and was used to walking through that door."

As Margaret had told us, Maureen was charming, greeting us in a warm and welcoming way. "Would you like to see some of the rooms?" she asked.

Of course we did.

Maureen took us into the hall where her family from long ago had dined and heard the coach-and-four coming down the entrance lane. She also showed us other rooms, including the drawing room with the gilt-framed mirror that had swallowed the gentleman ghost.

"I think you will be interested in seeing the cellar," Maureen said. "The foundation of the original fifteenth-century tower is down there." She led the way down the stairs into the darkness below.

The cellar looked as though it would be a perfect place for a ghost to haunt. The rough stone walls were streaked with lime and mold, and the massive oak beams in the ceiling were threateningly low.

"Here is the base of the original tower," Maureen explained, "destroyed by Cromwell over three hundred years ago on his devastating trek through the Irish countryside."

Then she pointed to the wall across from us.

"We have been told that the blood of one of Cromwell's men is on that wall," she said.

I was curious to see what seventeenth-century blood looked like, so I carefully made my way over the uneven floor to the bloodstained surface.

As I stared at a dark smudge on one of the stones, something else caught my attention. I sensed a definite presence next to me. I looked, and though no one was there, I still felt something standing very near, almost touching me.

I froze for a moment, then turned quickly and hurried back to Charles, Margaret, and Maureen—and told them I had just encountered a ghost, perhaps the ghost of the soldier whose blood was on the wall.

Margaret smiled, knowing that she had another ghost story to add to her tales of Maureen's haunted home.

THE MENACING MOTTE

The Motte House

When I think of Ireland, it brings back thoughts of ghosts and mottes. Ghosts are diaphanous, I have heard, but mottes are definitely not. In fact, they are solid, flat-topped mounds—built by the twelfth-century Norman invaders on which to erect their wooden towers.

Deep within these mottes (I would guess) live leprechauns, those famous creatures of Irish lore.

We once climbed a motte in a meadow near Cahir, in County Tipperary. Called Knockgraffon Motte, it is probably more than fifty feet in height, with sides just short of vertical. Yet, that day, we suddenly felt the urge to climb.

Since there was no pathway to the top, we crawled up, hanging onto grass and weeds. Well worth the crawl, since on this sunny day the view from the flattened top was breathtaking. Across the meadow, we saw the ruined tower of a castle built by the Butlers in Tudor times. And in another direction was a view down to the faraway River Suir. We left the motte top reluctantly, and, on the way down, slipped and slid on the grassy slope.

But the motte that interested us most was in an isolated place that took almost the whole afternoon to find. We were curious to see it because, over six centuries ago, James Butler, the first Earl of Ormond, had died in a stone tower that crowned it, and there was a good possibility that he had been one of Charles's ancestors. James had received the title when he was twenty-three, just ten years before his death.

The year before that, he had married King Edward II's niece, Eleanor de Bohun. So James died titled, leaving a noble wife and a very young son.

In anticipation of seeing the motte, I wrote to the owner of the estate on which it stood, to present my request. Her lawyer answered, writing that she (the owner) had died quite recently, and that it would be inconvenient for us to visit the place, since no one would be in residence.

No matter. We were still eager to see the motte on which James Butler had died.

After many wrong turns on country roads, we finally found the estate. It looked somewhat unfriendly, with its locked front gate and not a soul in sight. We found an entrance in the back that led to the estate manager's house, whose muddy forecourt was festooned with a pair of peacocks, plus chickens and other fowl.

The manager, after hearing our request to see the motte, took us through a gate and left us in a melancholy grove of trees through which we could see the outlines of a large and lonely house. The motte rose on our right. Unlike the smooth, green grass of sunlit Knockgraffon, this motte was rough with gloomy plants, including nettles.

The slope was so steep, and the possible route to the top so forbidding, that we quickly decided it was not worth the climb. Mark Bence–Jones, in his 1978 *Burke's Guide to Country Houses, Volume I, Ireland*, had written that, on this estate, some of the walls of an old Butler castle remained on the mound behind the house's garden. But from where we stood, we could not see the top of the motte and thus find out whether any stones from a medieval tower still remained.

Something besides the menacing motte held us back from exploring farther: I felt like an intruder. Also, a nearby rushing stream made me afraid to go too near its bank, lest I slip into its fast and noisy flow. A peacock shrieked. Wind blew through the branches of the trees, making a mysterious moan.

The hour was late. Our hotel was miles away. And we were tired. Then I remembered something else Bence–Jones had written about the house—that in the paneled dining room, one of the family portraits had the “strange habit of coming down from the wall and depositing itself by thc fireplace opposite,” always at the time of death of an important member of the family.

Since the last lady owner had recently died, the dining-room ghost was undoubtedly around to move the portrait again. Could it be willing us to stay away? I didn’t really want to find out. And as we hurried through the grove of trees, I definitely felt something push my back.

A WAIL IN THE WOODS

Suirview House

"Over the river and through the woods" goes the well-known verse. One day in County Tipperary, the river was the River Suir, and the woods was a dense woods just beyond the entrance gate of an elegant country house, now an inn. The house was an excellent example of fine eighteenth-century architecture. It was three stories high, with a beautiful bow front, and it sat on a wide lawn with the woods forming a perfect backdrop to it. I was soon to find out that this was a most unforgettable place to stay.

Charles and I had had an early dinner in town, ten miles away, and arrived at the inn just before dark. We were met at the front door by the lady of the house, who greeted us and led us up a handsome curved stairway to our room on the second floor. The guest room was spacious, with windows overlooking the lawn and, beyond, the woods we had just come through.

Our hostess explained in her lilting Irish voice, "My husband and I will be gone this evening, and you will be on your own. In fact, you are our only guests tonight. If you need anything, please let our daughter know. She'll be studying in her room on the top floor, where our family quarters are. There will be a fire in the library fireplace, and plenty of books and magazines for you to read. I trust that you will have a very pleasant time."

"Indeed, we will!" I said. "We look forward to spending a lovely evening in your delightful home."

And we did.

Sitting together on a cushiony couch in front of the library fireplace—with the soft flames dancing before us and the smell of burning peat scenting the room—was my idea of heaven. On a big round table in the center of the room were piles of magazines and books to read, as well as homemade cookies on an antique plate.

That evening, it was fun imagining that this great house was our very own.

When we reluctantly retired to our room, the time was about midnight, and I fell into a most relaxing sleep. It must have been an hour or two later that I suddenly awoke. An unearthly, eerie wail—neither human nor animal—pierced the cold, black air outside the open window of our room. A weird and mournful moan, as though a satanic creature were suffering in the fires of Hell, the wail came from the entrance woods.

I was paralyzed with fright, but then it stopped, and I was able to resume my sleep, accompanied by wild and strange dreams.

The next morning, I told Charles about the awful sound I had heard in the wee hours of the night. When we went downstairs to have breakfast, I told our hosts about hearing the supernatural wail coming from the woods.

"It was the most horrible sound I've ever heard," I said. "Did you hear it, too?"

"NO," our host replied emphatically. "I heard nothing like that!" "Nor I," said his wife.

Their teenage daughter had been helping with the breakfast, and when her parents left the room, she looked at us shyly and whispered under her breath, "I heard it. We *all* heard it, but they are afraid to speak of it. The sound you heard was a banshee! No one wants to admit hearing her. She is the harbinger of death."

GWENDOLYN

CAHIR CASTLE

One of the reasons that Charles and I like to travel to Ireland is to attend a five-day Butler family reunion, which happens every three years, and is attended by more than a hundred relatives from around the world.

The first member of the family to set foot on the Emerald Isle was a Norman who arrived in the late twelfth century, almost a hundred years after the Normans invaded England in 1066. This first member's last name was not Butler but Walter, and his given name was Theobald. By 1185, King Henry II of England had given Theobald Walter the title of "Chief Butler of Ireland," a title to be held by Theobald's heirs in perpetuity. To remind the future monarchs of England of this title, Theobald's heirs expediently changed their surname from Walter to Butler. Thus, Butler became an Irish name as well as an English one.

At Butler reunions, the family members congregate in County Kilkenny, in the south-central part of Ireland, to see places of Butler interest there and in adjacent counties. One day, our family group visited the huge Butler castle at Cahir, in County Tipperary. This castle has the distinction of being the only Irish castle captured in 1599 by the dashing earl of Essex, a favorite of Queen Elizabeth I.

I always think of Errol Flynn, who took the role of Essex in the movie *The Private Lives of Elizabeth and Essex*. At home, I am reminded of Essex's capturing Cahir Castle as I walk past a seventeenth-century Irish engraving of the event, which we have hanging in our living room—an odd, though dramatic, choice of subject matter for a living room.

Cahir Castle sits on a rocky isle in the fast-flowing River Suir. The castle still has its impressive keep, curtain walls, courtyards, and medieval hall. And it was here, in an almost deserted corner of the castle's hall, that we met an elderly Butler gentleman from Wales.

For some reason, while we talked, I thought of ghosts, perhaps because we had just descended a dark, winding stair in the keep, which reminded me of the winding stair in Dromoland Castle, where a ghost may have lurked.

As our Welsh Butler relative was describing his own house in Wales, I blurted out, "Have you ever seen a ghost?"

"A ghost? Oh, yes," Mr. Butler exclaimed. "There is, of course, Gwendolyn."

Then he proceeded to tell us about this lady ghost: "She lives in my house, and is quite shy, you know, so I see her only from time to time, usually at the end of a rather long hall. She seems to float into view in her long white gown, then slowly fades away. Gwendolyn is an important part of my family, and has been in my house for many years. I would miss her if she ever decided to leave."

At that moment, Maura Butler came up behind us to announce that the lecture on the Butlers of Cahir Castle was about to begin. Charles and I turned to greet her and say that we were eager to hear the lecture. And when we turned back, Mr. Butler from Wales had disappeared.

On the remaining days of the reunion, we looked for him but never found him.

Finally, on the last day, I asked Miss Agnes Butler, who was in charge of the reunion's affairs, to give us the full name and address of the Butler gentleman from Wales.

"Oh, I'm sorry," Miss Agnes replied. "There was no Butler gentleman from Wales at *this* reunion. Three years ago, there was Mr. Geoffrey Butler, but, alas, he died."

THE GHOST AT BALLYCONRA

BALLYCONRA

As far as I know, there has been only one titled Butler ghost. Mark Bence–Jones, in his *Burke's Guide to Country Houses, Volume I, Ireland*, names the ghost as that of Edmund Butler, twelfth Viscount Mountgarret and first Earl of Kilkenny.

Edmund Butler lived in Ballyconra House, an elegant, early eighteenth-century house on an extensive estate north of Kilkenny. The titles and the estate came to him in 1793, when his father died after partaking of an excess of cider and strawberries.

Sadly, Edmund went mad by 1799. However, he continued to live on in Ballyconra House until he died in 1846. His ghost has often been seen in this handsome house.

One dark and rainy day, in the late afternoon, Charles and I decided to visit Ballyconra House. No one was living there then, we were told, since the house was being renovated. By the time we arrived, the workmen had left for the day and their ladders and scaffolds were in place on the main floor. The only people remaining in the house were two Irish lasses from the neighborhood.

"May we show you around?" they asked.

"Yes, please do," Charles replied, and he mentioned that he was a Butler, and possibly even descended from the Butlers who had built the house.

They gave us a leisurely tour of the downstairs, pointing out such things as the decorative plasterwork ceiling, which was being restored. We strolled through the drawing room, the front hall, the study, and then into the dining room, which was divided into two parts by a large arch. One of the young ladies pointed to the area beyond the arch and told us, in a soft voice, "They say it is haunted in there."

After waiting a few minutes and seeing nothing spectral, the other young woman sighed and said, "You came all the way from America to see your family ghost, and he didn't even come out to greet you. Well, we have one more opportunity."

The two of them took us into a dark back hall, where a wooden staircase rose to a landing and into the shadows above.

Our guides knew all about the ghost of Edmund Butler, and one of them confessed, "We were so curious about his ghost that, once, we stayed here after dark to see if it might come floating up and down these stairs, for it is here that he is most often seen. But 'twas all in vain, for the ghostly gentleman never did appear that night."

The other young lady added, "They say he is always dressed like a nineteenth-century lord, and he wears a tall silk hat."

Unhappily, we saw no sign of Edmund that afternoon, either ascending or descending the stairs. But later, a thought occurred to me. If Edmund Butler were really in residence, surely he would have sought refuge in the attic at the upper reaches of the stair, until the restoration work was done. Then, when the new owners occupied the house, he would return to haunt the staircase and the dining room, dressed, as always, in his finest nineteenth-century clothes.

By the time Charles and I left Ballyconra House, the rain had stopped and the sun had come out. Low in the sky, the sun cast long shadows across the lawn. We decided to leave by the back door and walk around the house to our car, which we had parked in front.

At the side of the house, I looked up and observed how tall it was—with its gable and chimney, which added to the height. In the gable was an attic window that caught the light from the setting sun. There, I was startled to see a man's face whose eyes stared at me, but only for one second.

When I took a step forward, the face disappeared.

CASTLEMEAD

Castlemead House

One weekend, Charles and I were houseguests at a wonderful eighteenth-century country house in County Kilkenny. Our host and his wife were both writers, as were the original owners of the house, and that weekend there was a third houseguest, who was also a writer. Both our host and fellow houseguest shared the same old-fashioned, but distinguished, given name of Hubert. We have seldom spent such an entertaining time as when we were in their company.

On Saturday, we drove the two Huberts here and there around the countryside. They rode in the backseat, calling themselves "Hubert Major" and "Hubert Minor," while Charles and I sat in front, listening to their amusing tales. We learned that sunny afternoon that it was the custom, at least in days gone by, for owners of country houses to make unannounced calls on neighboring friends and acquaintances. Hubert Major told us of one such teatime call.

"We decided to visit a rather pretentious husband and wife in County Clare," he said in a serious tone. "Distant relatives, you know. We were seated in the very proper drawing room of their quite sedate abode. After the servant brought the tea tray to the table and the lady of the house was starting the formal ritual, a chicken entered the room. It fluttered onto the table and bounced around the cups and pots and scones, making itself quite at home as it clucked noisily—with everyone pretending that it was not even there."

Hubert Major's tale reminded me that a fine country house called Castlemead was nearby. Since visiting such houses without an invitation was still acceptable, this was a perfect opportunity for me to see it. Castlemead was said to have an old castle tower next to it.

When I suggested to Hubert Major that we pay a visit, he smiled his approval and told us, "I haven't been there since the present owner—an Englishman—moved in. As we are already in the vicinity, Hubert Minor and I would be delighted to go with you."

As with most estates, this manor house was approached by a long entrance road, down which I saw a crenellated, bow-fronted façade. Behind the house, apparently attached to it, there was a tall castle tower. This was typical in Ireland: an eighteenth- or nineteenth-century big house built onto a castle tower usually constructed three or four centuries earlier.

When we rapped on the door, the owner came and invited us into the drawing room. He was a good-looking man in his early forties, who informed us that he lived alone, raised dogs, and was planning to sell the place and return to England. There was a certain chillness in the drawing room, as though a curtain of silence had dropped in with us—the uninvited guests.

"I noticed you have a castle tower behind your lovely house," I said, hoping to raise the curtain. "I wonder if we might see it. I am quite interested in buildings of that period."

To which he politely obliged, though with some hesitation. I sensed that he might not be at ease with strangers arriving in the afternoon without an invitation.

Down a hall we went, following our host, until we reached a door on the right. To our surprise, when he opened it, all we saw was a drop of about ten feet to a dirt floor inside an empty square tower. There were a million cobwebs clinging desperately to the gray stone walls. I immediately exclaimed, "There must be a ghost in here!"

"Absolutely *not*," said our host emphatically. "I know all about ghosts. In fact, I saw one when I was a houseguest at Rossenarra. I met it in an upstairs hall. But here, at *my* place, there are *no* ghosts!"

I, of course, made no comment, but was sure that if there were such things as ghosts, they would certainly take up residence here.

We soon left, after declining his rather reluctantly offered tea. While driving away, the two Huberts explained to us that since the estate was up for sale, having a resident ghost was one of the worst things an owner could wish for.

"If a house is known to have a ghost, its selling price will drop precipitously," said Hubert Minor. And Hubert Major agreed.

But I said to Charles afterward, "Anyone visiting this Englishman's Irish house will immediately suspect that a ghost or two live in that tower."

THE BELATED VISITOR

CARRICK CASTLE

One afternoon, as we stood with other Butler family members on the lawn in front of Carrick Castle, in County Tipperary, Charles and I heard about a royal scandal in the Butler family.

Addressing our group was a distinguished lecturer, who told us, "The man who built this handsome Elizabethan mansion was Thomas Butler, the father of Queen Elizabeth I's only child."

This startling statement came as no surprise to the audience of Butlers. They already knew that Elizabeth Tudor and Thomas Butler had had an affair that produced a son. The son was named Piers FitzThomas Butler, and his father gave him extensive estates, treating him more generously than he did his other illegitimate sons.

Thomas Butler was the eldest son of the ninth Earl of Ormond and the Countess of Desmond. Elizabeth Tudor was the daughter of King Henry VIII and Anne Boleyn, making

Elizabeth and Thomas distant cousins. They were two years apart, and both had been brought up in the English court, so, of course, they were well acquainted.

Thomas was known from his early years as "Black Tom," possibly because of his black hair, his dark complexion, or to differentiate him from another well-known noble, Sir Thomas Wyatt, who was called "White Tom." I picture Black Tom as a high-spirited, popular young man.

Members of the Butler family and others believe that Elizabeth conceived a child with Black Tom when she was 20, five years before she became Queen of England. In her later years, she is known to have referred to him as "my black husband."

Black Tom spent most of his young life in England, but eventually settled in Ireland, where he possessed vast tracts of land. After his father died in 1545, Black Tom, at age 15, took over these estates and was given his father's title, thus becoming the tenth Earl of Ormond.

One of Black Tom's Irish estates was the manor of Carrick, with its fine old castle built over a century earlier, on the banks of the River Suir. Carrick Castle soon became Black Tom's favorite residence, surpassing even his huge castle in Kilkenny. When he was in his early thirties, he began building a mansion onto Carrick Castle (sometimes called Ormond Castle, because of his title) in order to provide an elegant place for Queen Elizabeth to stay. But he was always disappointed. She never came.

Nevertheless, he did not let the possibility of the queen's visit stand in the way of his three marriages or his liaisons with various women. It has been estimated that Black Tom fathered at least a dozen offspring. Still, I believe his heart was always with his early love, Elizabeth. She must have known this, too. In the mansion can be found the initials of Black Tom intertwined with those of Queen Elizabeth, done in plasterwork.

Charles and I have visited Carrick Castle several times. Once, with a group of thirty Butlers, we arrived on an excursion boat that had wound its way through the verdant countryside along the banks of the River Suir—a twenty-mile cruise from Waterford. When we disembarked at Carrick Castle, it was late afternoon, and a group of local ladies welcomed us with tea in the courtyard.

On another visit, after entering Carrick Castle by the front door, Charles and I came into the luxurious mansion Black Tom had built in the 1560s. We passed the doorway to the charter room off to our right, where a collection of royal charters on parchment—granted to members of the titled Ormond Butlers, starting in the mid-seventeenth century—was on display.

Because the hour was late, we continued our visit by going to the floor above, where the most important, most highly decorated room of the mansion is located. This is the long gallery, a truly impressive room created by Black Tom for the visit of his Queen. We entered the gallery at its west end and looked down the great hall, which is more than a hundred feet in length—the entire length of the upper floor.

There are many windows along the outer wall, other windows overlooking the inner court, and tall windows at each end of the room. Plenty of sunlight enters the gallery during the middle of sunny days. But now, in the late afternoon, the light was muted, though strong enough for us to see the elaborate plasterwork decorations on the walls and ceiling.

They were lavishly decorated with Tudor symbols that would have impressed Queen Elizabeth, if she had ever visited. Above the windows, we saw a wide plasterwork frieze decorated with the queen's monogram, Tudor roses, and portraits of Queen Elizabeth and her half brother, King Edward VI.

Charles decided to stroll down the hall observing not only the frieze, but also the beautifully executed plasterwork ceiling. He paused halfway down, in front of a fireplace with an overmantel featuring a bust of Queen Elizabeth encircled by a laurel wreath.

I was interested in another fireplace near the west end of the gallery. There, on a stone overmantel, was the Butler family coat of arms, maybe three feet high, with two griffin supporters, Latin inscriptions, and myriad Butler family symbols—all carved by Irish artists.

Then I saw a woman sitting on a chair in the far corner of the room. She was dressed in Elizabethan costume, so I assumed she must have been a guide waiting for a special group of tourists to arrive. Her dress was gray with a voluminous skirt and slashed sleeves, the fabric richly patterned. Around her neck, there was a pleated ruff. Her face was as white as the gallery's plasterwork. As I walked down the hall to join Charles, who was still looking at the overmantel with the portrait of Queen Elizabeth, I was surprised to see the resemblance between the face on the overmantel and the face of the woman in the far corner of the long gallery.

"Charles, do you see the woman sitting over there?" I asked.

"What woman?"

"The one in costume," I pointed, "by the window."

"You must be seeing things," he said. "There is no woman there. No one is in the gallery but you and me."

At that moment, the woman arose slowly and gracefully. She stood tall, waited, then started gliding toward us. But as soon as she stepped in front of a window, I gasped. I could see the window right through her!

Then she gradually faded away. First her dress, then her ruff, until all that was left was her very white face, as immovable as the portrait bust of Elizabeth above the fireplace.

When her face disappeared, I managed to say to Charles, "I just saw the ghost of Queen Elizabeth!"

She had come at last to be with Black Tom, who had died here in Carrick Castle almost four hundred years ago.

Suddenly, the gallery had grown strangely cold. I was trembling at the thought of what I had seen.

A TALE OF TWO ABBEYS

Kilcooley Abbey

I have had unforgettable things happen to me near two deserted abbeys. One abbey is in England, and the other on the Emerald Isle.

The one in Ireland was built by the Cistercian order of monks in County Tipperary. It is called Kilcooley Abbey, and was founded in the time of Henry II by a famous Irish king, Dónal Mór O'Brien.

Kilcooley Abbey has had its share of problems with fires and plunder, but it is still in remarkably good condition. The sixteenth century saw the suppression of monasteries by Henry VIII, who gave Kilcooley Abbey and its lands to the then powerful Butlers. They held it for many years, so naturally we were interested in this former Butler property.

It is not easy to reach Kilcooley Abbey. One must first turn into a walled demesne, then drive down a long road through dense woods, and finally turn onto a narrow lane through more dense woods. At the end of the lane is a low wall with a stile.

From the top of the stile, one can see a vast, green field. Sitting in the middle of the field, a hundred yards away, Kilcooley Abbey looks like a miniature architectural model resting on a pool table covered in bright-green baize. Off to the left, there is a dovecote believed to date from the sixteenth century, and one of the last left in Ireland.

A walking path heads directly from the stile to the abbey church's north transept door, which is the main entrance now.

The last time that Charles and I visited Kilcooley Abbey, we entered by this door and were soon at the crossing beneath the tower. To our right was the roofless nave. To our left, the chancel, with the beautifully carved tomb of Piers Fitz Oge Butler. His stone effigy, dressed in knight's armor, lies peacefully under the east window.

But the most interesting part of Kilcooley Abbey, for me, is the stone wall that separates the south transept from the sacristy. Here are carvings of the Crucifixion, of St. Christopher, and, my favorite, of a mermaid holding a mirror while being admired by two friendly fish. This mermaid, in centuries past, had symbolized vanity, and she was shown to warn women against this vice.

I was in a cheerful, exhilarated mood when we last left Kilcooley Abbey and walked down the path back to the stile.

Then, without warning, I felt as though I were being pushed, and I fell flat on my face. Fortunately, I was wearing a wool turtleneck sweater, wool pants, and leather gloves. But the fall came as a great shock after our pleasant visit to the abbey.

I thought, perhaps the ghost of a Cistercian monk disapproved of my makeup. And I had just touched up my lipstick in the nave, holding a mirror!

The second unforgettable thing happened to me by Whitby Abbey, in England. Charles and I had driven around the country in a rental car looking for places of special interest to us.

ENGLAND

- (A) Inn at Hutton
- (B) Mermaid Inn
- (C) Swan Stoke
- (D) Whitby Abbey

The year before, we had talked our two mothers into traveling to England together. Charles's mother had always dreamed of going to Yorkshire and visiting Robin Hood's Bay, the home of her great-grandfather Thornton. My mother had visited England several times before and was delighted to go again.

During the month our mothers were there, they traveled to Robin Hood's Bay, where they stayed in a quaint Victorian hotel on the top of a hill. On their return, they often reminisced about walking down the steep hill from the hotel to buy fish and chips from a vendor on the waterfront. They always mentioned that the fish and chips were served in newspaper cones.

Charles and I wanted to see where our mothers had stayed, so we decided to put Robin Hood's Bay on our itinerary. Since it was so near Whitby, we decided to go to Whitby first, especially to see the ruins of the abbey. Before we left home, I had read in Antony D. Hippisley Coxe's book, *Haunted Britain*, that Whitby Abbey was "a ghost hunter's paradise."

Whitby Abbey

The most famous ghost of all, he wrote, was St. Hilda, who was often seen in one of the highest windows of the abbey church, wearing a shroud.

When we reached the abbey, I spent some time looking at the highest windows, always with my eyes open for the ghost of St. Hilda. Failing to see even a glimpse of her, I started walking across the parking lot to our car. The parking lot was perfectly flat. There was nothing there to stumble on. Yet, I fell on my face!

Fortunately, a woman who saw me fall rushed over to check if I had broken any bones. She told us that there was a clinic at Robin Hood's Bay, our destination anyhow.

At Robin Hood's Bay, we stopped at the Victorian hotel where our mothers had stayed, and I limped in to learn the location of the clinic. I was amazed to find the hotel's pub filled with local folk, because it was only eleven in the morning. I told them that I had taken a bad fall at Whitby Abbey and needed to have a clinic treat my wounds from the fall.

I was also tempted to tell them a ghost had pushed me down, but I decided it would be better to get to the clinic as soon as possible.

And as I left the crowded pub, I overheard a patron say, "St. Hilda."

REMEMBERING RYE

The Mermaid Inn

While living in Spain, we traveled beyond the Spanish border, through France, then across the English Channel to "Merry Olde England," the land of my ancestors and home to multitudes of ghosts, I had read. We had never been there before.

Our first night in England, we stayed at the early fifteenth-century Mermaid Inn, in Rye, a perfect place to experience English medieval atmosphere. Our large room had diamond-paned windows, a beamed ceiling, and dark paneling. As I remember, so did the dining room.

But what I remember most while dining there that night were the other diners, who were drinking Spanish sherry throughout their meals! I had always thought of sherry as an aperitif, taken at cocktail time.

Another surprise came the next morning, when the door to our room opened, and, without knocking, an elderly maid entered carrying a huge tray with a big pot of tea and other breakfast delights. We had not ordered tea to be brought to our room, certainly not while we were still asleep. And we drank coffee, never tea. But in the spirit of the occasion, that day we did.

Later that morning, when we were about to walk around the town, we met a young housemaid in the hall outside our room.

"Did you see the ghost?" she asked expectantly.

"Well, *no*," I replied. "A *ghost*?"

"Yes, there is one," she said in a hushed voice. "And he appears in your room from time to time."

She had simply wondered if we had seen him. In a way, I was sorry that he had failed to appear.

That night, moonlight shone in the windows of our room so brightly, I simply had to leave the comfort of our great four-poster bed to see Rye illuminated by it.

As I stood by an open window savoring the scene, out of the corner of my eye, I saw a pale shape on the far side of the room. I turned quickly to face the shape. It moved slowly back and forth, then suddenly disappeared.

Quivering from head to toe, I rushed back to bed and pulled the covers over my head.

The next day, as we drove west to Brighton, I told Charles what had happened during the night. He said I had probably seen a curtain moving in a draft.

To this day, I clearly remember there were no curtains in our room at the Mermaid Inn.

A FLIGHT IN THE NIGHT

The Inn at Hutton

Another English ghost that we heard about was in the town of Hutton, in the west. We went to Hutton because a distant ancestor of mine had lived there in the eighteenth century and we wished to see his home, which was now an inn, or had been until recently and was being renovated when we visited.

The owner kindly took us all over the property—to the classical folly on the side lawn, which once served my ancestor as a library; to the spacious and sunny dining room; and upstairs to the most important bedroom of the inn. Then the owner showed us an adjoining, narrow staircase that climbed up a central tower.

"At the top of this tower," he explained, "is a small room, which I recently allowed one of our dining room waiters to use as his bedchamber. It is a fine room—private and quiet."

"Well," he continued, "the waiter did not spend even one night up there. After he had gone to bed in the little room, he was awakened abruptly. There, at the foot of his bed, was a female ghost who stared at him with penetrating eyes. Within a second, the waiter leapt from his bed, dashed down the stairs, and out of the inn. He stayed just long enough to tell me what he had seen, and that he was *never* coming back. Of course, I have never seen the lady ghost, but I am sure the waiter did."

Apparently, this intrigued Charles, for he asked the owner if we might see the room at the top of the tower.

"Yes, of course," the owner replied. "Let me show you the way."

The stairs to the top of the tower looked dark and steep, so I decided not to accompany them. Instead, I wandered leisurely around the grand bedroom, finally pausing in front of a tall mirror that reflected the entrance to the tower stair.

I was thinking of my ancestor who used to live in this house. Did his descendants live here, too? Then, without warning, as I stared in the mirror, I saw a lady standing behind me at the entrance to the stairs. She was dressed in black.

Her face instantly reminded me of a small daguerreotype of a nineteenth-century aunt of mine. When I turned around for a better look, the lady in black had disappeared.

But she left behind a distinctive scent of lavender.

SWAN STOKE

Swan Stoke

Swan Stoke is a centuries-old house in the English hinterland. That, in itself, should make it a perfect candidate for a haunted house. It belonged to a branch of my family as far back as the late fifteenth century, when an ancestor moved from Somerset to the Cotswolds, married the daughter of the local lord, took the lord's title when he died, and lived in Swan Stoke—or so the story goes. The first member of my branch of the family to visit the place was my mother.

Well, she did not exactly visit it, since the house had been deserted for some time before she arrived, and she only saw the house from about fifty yards away. Mother had flown to England to be the guest of Darlene, a college friend of hers—and the two of them had decided to find Swan Stoke while they were driving around the Cotswold Hills. This house was high on Mother's list of places to be sure to see.

Late on a cold and drizzly day, they finally discovered the entrance lane to Swan Stoke. After driving along it for more than a quarter mile, Mother caught sight of the house ahead. She suddenly commanded Darlene to *stop!* As Mother described it to me, "The house all at once appeared out of nowhere, a dark gray hulk, three-stories high with Gothic gables, and a decidedly unwelcoming air. I was too frightened to have Darlene drive any closer to that ominous-looking place. Darlene agreed, quickly turned the car around, and we never looked back."

A few years later, on a trip to England, Charles and I decided to see Swan Stoke for ourselves, since Mother's description had intrigued—rather than discouraged—me. We arrived at the entrance lane on a somewhat more promising, but still overcast, day.

The lane was narrow and seemingly endless, but we finally saw the house ahead. Unlike Mother and Darlene, we drove on until we reached it, and parked nearby. We could tell from the dark, uncurtained windows that no one was living there. Walking around the house, we found an archway with a stone wyvern perched on top, the same wyvern that appears on our family's coat of arms.

Then we encountered a cheerful farmer who said he owned the place, as he gestured toward the house, a nearby stable, a few sheds, and other outbuildings.

"Over there I store my machinery, and over here is where I store the grain. But the house is empty. Would you like to see inside? I am thinking of selling it."

We assumed he meant to sell only the house, and to keep ownership of the surrounding lands he farmed. But who would buy only the house, encircled, as it was, by farm activity? And did he think we were prospective buyers?

Inside, all was dusty, lifeless, and a bit cluttered with odds and ends. The most impressive part was the kitchen, which had a huge fireplace that stretched across one side of the room. The fireplace reminded me of a wide but shallow stage, the long wood lintel like the top of a proscenium arch.

How I would like to design a set for one of Shakespeare's tragedies, I thought, to be performed right here.

After we had explored the rooms downstairs, the farmer asked whether we would like to see the upper levels. Though curious, all at once I was afraid to attempt the climb, fearful that I might crash through a weakened stair tread or a rotting floorboard on the floors above. Besides, I was growing anxious to leave the shadowy interior of the Swan Stoke house.

Before we left, Charles took photos of the rooms on the ground floor and quite a few of the outdoors, including one of the whole south side of the house, the only side that was unobstructed by farm machinery and trees.

When we returned to the United States, we spent an evening going through the newly developed photographs of our England trip. At last we came to the ones Charles had taken at Swan Stoke—the kitchen fireplace, the stone wyvern on the arch, the friendly farmer, the stable, and the south side of the house. On seeing this last print, I gasped, "What is that in the window?" Whereas all the other windows in the house were dark, one window on the second floor was filled with an odd, white shape.

"It must be a reflection of some sort," Charles explained. "Perhaps a cloud."

I prefer to believe that it was a ghost, whose presence had made Mother and me so very uncomfortable.

SPAIN

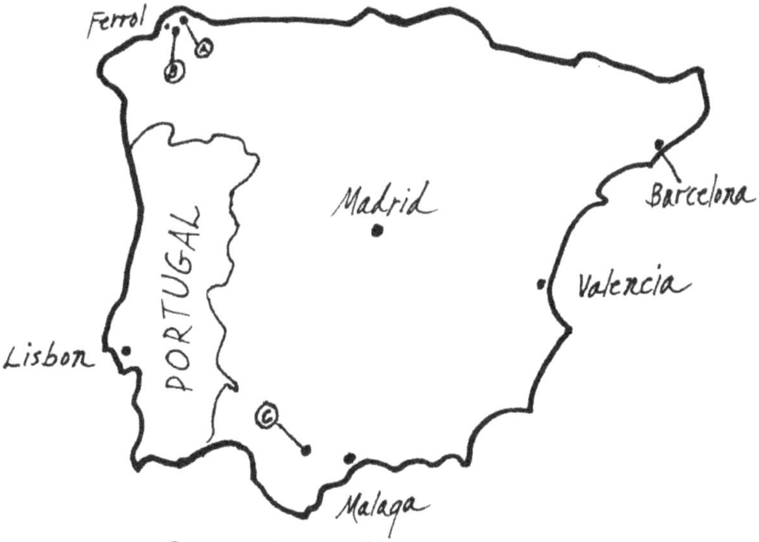

Ⓐ Moeche Castle

Ⓑ Narahío Castle

Ⓒ A Cave in Spain

A CAVE IN SPAIN

A Cave in Spain

There is a remote place we visited in southern Spain that still makes my heart grow cold. The time was winter, and Charles and I stood shivering by the entrance to a cave in the mountains, miles from anywhere.

We were alone—neither a tourist nor anyone else in sight. We had read that in this cave were several prehistoric murals, and since prehistoric art interested both of us, we were eager to see them.

But a locked iron gate at the entrance to the cave prevented us from reaching them.

Then we noticed a small cottage down the hill, where we found a man who seemed to live alone. After asking him about the cave, he mumbled sullenly that he did have the key.

Apparently, we had disrupted his siesta, yet he still agreed to let us in the cave and even be our guide.

When we reached the entrance, he unlocked the iron gate and we entered with the great anticipation of seeing some prehistoric art. Once inside, however, he relocked the gate. I was not pleased, but understood that no one should be allowed inside without a guide, and, apparently, ours was the only one around.

He lighted a lantern, which didn't please me, either. Only one lantern—fueled with what seemed to me dangerous kerosene. We were not off to a propitious start.

While the outside temperature had been cold, inside the cave was pleasantly warm. Unfortunately, this welcoming warmth was the only positive thing we were experiencing. Our guide continued to be morose. The lantern was dim. The narrow walkway rose, then dropped, as though it were riding the waves at sea. And it was slippery with mud, as well.

As we slipped and slid along, we kept asking the man, "Where is the prehistoric art?" And he kept telling us, "*Más allá.*" Farther on.

The path seemed endless, and the murals just beyond our reach. I was growing apprehensive and was starting to be alarmed, for we had been walking (no, sliding) for at least half an hour, I was sure. I felt that we were now deep inside the cave.

Thoughts started pouring through my mind. What if the flame in the lantern went out and left us in total darkness? What if the guide dropped his key in the muddy walkway, and we could not find it? What if we were never able to escape from this frightful cave?

The guide suddenly stopped and pointed to a small, indistinct painting on a side wall. Prehistoric art, at last! Charles quickly brought out his camera and started to take flash photos while I stepped aside to give him more room. In doing this, I happened to look down the walkway ahead. There, for an instant, I saw a hooded figure, six feet tall, wearing a cape that reached the ground.

At that very moment, the guide said, "*Mi abuelo...*," which means "my grandfather," and that is all I heard him say, because I panicked on the spot. I had seen the ghost of our guide's grandfather, and I had to get out of this cave immediately. Charles told me later that he had never seen me in such a state of pure panic.

We rushed back, following our slippery route in record time. Outside the cave, when I finally caught my breath and was sitting in our car, I said, "I think I saw the ghost of our guide's grandfather! I heard him say it was his *abuelo*!"

"No," Charles explained. "He only told us that his grandfather was the first to discover the cave's murals. But I can see how—in your frightened state in that dark cave—you could easily have imagined seeing a ghost."

After a long pause, Charles added, "Well, our guide was quite relieved to leave the cave, too. On the way out, he also told me he had seen the apparition that lives there."

THE MYSTERIOUS CASTLE OF MOECHE

Moeche Castle

Charles and I devoted a whole day to visiting the Spanish castle of Moeche. Even though we had heard that it was within twenty miles of our country house in northwest Spain, no one seemed to know exactly where it was. None of our Spanish friends—not even our country maid, Juana—could tell us how to find it, although all of them had heard of Moeche and knew it was somewhere in the hills.

The day we chose to find the castle was drizzly. The Spanish word for drizzle is *llovizna.* But in Galicia (or at least in our part of Galicia) the local people call it *calabobos*. And that was definitely a calabobos day.

We did know the general direction to Moeche. After driving northeast into the hills, we wandered around on backcountry roads until we came upon an almost hidden valley. In the distance, we saw a castle tower rising above a grove of trees. It was Moeche Castle, we were sure.

After parking the car at the foot of the hillock on which the castle stood, we walked up a path to the old structure, which seemed to be remarkably well-preserved for a building from medieval times. The entrance was in the main tower. A drawbridge over the moat had once led to it.

Above the tower entrance was the coat of arms of Fernán Pérez de Andrade, who built the castle five hundred years ago, though it had been abandoned for over three hundred years. All this we found out later. That day, we only knew the castle's name.

As we walked through the thick wall of the entrance into the tower, we looked up and saw the ominous slot for the portcullis—the iron grill that closed off access when lowered. Inside, the tower rose over three stories high and had a window and a roof.

Another doorway led into the main part of the castle, which, unlike the tower, was open to the sky. Here were strong outer walls and a grassy courtyard surrounded by inner walls denoting where rooms had been.

When the lord of the castle was in residence, he would have lived on the floor above, away from the soldiers and servants, who stayed in the lower part. We could see the lord's fireplace high on a wall, still hanging there like a bat in a belfry.

After walking from room to room and around the courtyard, we finally spotted, in a corner of one room, a small round tower with a doorway that opened onto a dark spiral stair. In Spanish, a spiral stair is called a *caracol*, which also means "snail." Being curious, we decided to climb the castle's caracol—as you may have guessed it—at a snail's pace.

At the top of the stair, we stepped onto a narrow walkway that encircled the top of the outer castle walls. From here, we could look down to the courtyard and the empty rooms far below.

We followed the walkway until it entered a doorway in the thick wall of the main tower. Inside the tower was another doorway. It opened onto a stair that, unlike the caracol, went straight up to the roof of the tower. Here we found that the roof was rimmed with broken battlements. As we looked between the merlons, we could see the emerald-green countryside of the valley spread out before us. Alone on a castle tower: What could be more romantic!

The hour was growing late as we left the tower's roof in a cheerful mood, walking carefully down the steep stair, and then out into the drizzle, which had almost stopped.

A loud thump behind us made us jump. When we turned, we saw a large stone lying on the walkway. It had fallen off the tower—and I was very shaken. It could have easily landed on our heads.

We thanked our lucky stars, then quickly went down the spiral stair, through the main tower, and down the hill to our car.

On the drive home, we decided that something must have loosened the wayward stone. However, it occurred to me later that it could have been a ghost who did not want strangers disturbing his solitude, so he dropped the rock as a warning. After all, it came crashing down in a drizzle, not a storm.

IN THE RUINED TOWER OF NARAHÍO

Narahio Castle

In the mid-1950s, when Charles and I lived in Galicia, a region in northwest Spain, I seldom thought about ghosts. Perhaps I should have been more aware of the possibility of their existence, since we often drove off on weekends to remote and likely haunted places.

We especially enjoyed wandering around deserted monasteries and ruined castles, not only in Galicia, but also in nearby northern Portugal. It is possible that in all of these places there lurked unseen spirits, at least in the minds of those who believed in them.

Once, we took a fascinating, all-day hike with two Spanish friends, Alberto and Ramón, to visit the ruined castle of Narahío. We parked the car by the side of a narrow road at the top of a high ridge, and from there we could see far down in a valley to the top of the castle tower, which looked like a toy rising from a forest of green. Unfortunately, there were no roads to the castle then, but Alberto and Ramón found a shepherd boy who said he would show us the way.

For about two miles we hiked down the hillside on steep, winding paths through fields of cabbages and corn. At last, we came to a wooded valley, through which flowed a small, swift river crossed by a stone arch bridge. Our shepherd guide told us, in *gallego* (the local dialect that only our friends could understand), that on certain nights the people of the valley could hear the cries and shouts of medieval Spanish and Moorish warriors battling near the bridge. He called it a Roman bridge, as stone arch bridges were typically called in Galicia, where the Romans were active during the first three centuries of the Christian era.

The nearby ruin of the fourteenth-century castle was more interesting to me. It stood on a precipitous outcrop of rock. The Castle of Narahío had been abandoned over three hundred and fifty years earlier. Its tower still stood like a sentinel atop its rocky base, while its broken walls lay scattered down the slope.

We scrambled up the rocky slope and over the remains of Narahío's outer walls. Exhausted, I decided to rest while Charles and our two friends explored the ruined walls, climbing down to where they could see a river flowing at the base of the hill.

As I rested, I gazed up to the tower, where I noticed a window not far from the top. And I saw a face—a face looking down at me! Even though it lasted but a second, I still remember it clearly: a bearded face with blank eyes and a look that was expressionless but fierce. I turned away at once, startled by what I had just seen.

When Charles, Alberto, and Ramón returned, I could hardly wait to tell them about it. They all laughed and invited me to join them in investigating the ghost in the tower. I followed them and gingerly entered behind them, but none of us found any sign of a ghost—only the rough walls of an empty tower. Later, our friends often teased me about my seeing the ghost of Narahío.

After Charles and I left Spain and returned to live in the United States, Ramón sent us an old book about the medieval buildings of Galicia. In the book were descriptions and floor plans of many of the Galician castles, including Narahío. Its plan showed the square castle tower surrounded by a twelve-sided wall, and at the base of the rocky outcrop, a river identified as the *Río de Narahío*.

The big surprise was that a secret tunnel (a vaulted passageway, the old book called it) ran from the castle tower down through the rocky hill, all the way to the river. Those who lived in the castle—if they saw an enemy approaching—could escape down this tunnel to a waiting boat.

Had my bearded ghost escaped that way? Or was the fierce face only an illusion—caused by the sun and shadows on the window jamb, visible only at that moment of the day?

Your guess is as good as mine.

Names and Locations

Ballyconra House is 10 miles north of Kilkenny, County Kilkenny, Ireland.

Cahir Castle is in Cahir, County Tipperary, Ireland.

Carrick Castle is in Carrick-on-Suir, County Tipperary, Ireland.

Castlemead* is 15 miles southeast of Kilkenny, County Kilkenny, Ireland.

Cave in Spain is the Cueva de la Pileta, which is 20 miles southwest of Ronda, Malaga Province, in southern Spain.

Dromoland Castle is in County Clare, Ireland. It is 10 miles north of Shannon Airport.

Inn at Hutton is in Hutton, which is near Weston-super-Mare, Avon, on the west coast of England.

Kilcooley Abbey is 20 miles northeast of Cashel, County Tipperary, Ireland.

Kilkea Castle is near Castledermot, County Kildare, Ireland.

Maureen's Castle is 20 miles east of Kilkenny, County Kilkenny, Ireland. Maureen is not the real name of our friend.

Mermaid Inn is in Rye, East Sussex, on the south coast of England.

Moeche Castle is 15 miles northeast of Ferrol, La Coruña Province, Galicia, in northwest Spain.

Motte House* is 5 miles southwest of Thurles, County Tipperary, Ireland.

Narahío Castle is 10 miles east of Ferrol, La Coruña Province, Galicia, Spain.

Suirview* is 5 miles north of Cashel, County Tipperary, Ireland.

Swan Stoke* is 10 miles south of Stratford-upon-Avon, Warwickshire, England.

Whitby Abbey is on the east coast of England, near Whitby, North Yorkshire.

* In stories where the castle or house mentioned is privately owned, the names have been changed to respect the privacy of the owner.

About the Author

Rosemary Butler was married in the chapel at the Naval Academy, Annapolis, near the tomb of John Paul Jones. His spirit, she presumes, came to the wedding to wish the bride and groom a happy and adventurous life. This may have been her first encounter with a ghost—but not her last!

For twenty years, she accompanied her husband—a naval officer and civil engineer—to job sites on American bases in Alaska (before statehood), Spain, the Philippines, and the United States, where he was in charge of construction projects. This enabled them to travel extensively in Europe and Asia. Since living in Florida, they have traveled to Ireland a dozen times, as well as revisited England and Spain.

Rosemary Butler has been a librarian, a researcher of Italian Renaissance paintings, and a set designer for college and community theaters. Her most memorable sets were for the Third Company of *South Pacific*, which was performed at all major military bases in Alaska. She also wrote and produced a radio program for children during their residence there.

In college, at the University of Iowa, the University of Illinois, and Monmouth College, Rosemary studied set design, art history, and art. Photos of her art assemblages appear in *The Art of the Miniature*, by Jane Freeman, and two of Rosemary's paintings were chosen for an exhibition to mark the opening of the National Library in Manila.

More recently, she was the featured speaker at an international meeting of the Butler Society at Kilkenny Castle, in Ireland. She has written articles on early Irish history, published in England and Ireland.

www.ingramcontent.com/pod-product-compliance
Lightning Source LLC
Chambersburg PA
CBHW020505100426
42813CB00030B/3132/J
* 9 7 8 1 8 8 3 3 7 8 0 1 1 *